MINICK AND SIMPSON BLUE & WHITE

MINICK AND SIMPSON

Blue &

Living with Textiles You Love

Polly Minick and Laurie Simpson

Minick and Simpson Blue & White:
Living with Textiles You Love
© 2017 by Polly Minick and Laurie Simpson

Martingale®
19021 120th Ave. NE, Ste. 102
Bothell, WA 98011-9511 USA
ShopMartingale.com

Printed in China
22 21 20 19 18 17   8 7 6 5 4 3 2 1

Library of Congress Cataloging-in-Publication Data
is available upon request.

ISBN: 978-1-60468-868-9

MISSION STATEMENT

We empower makers who use fabric and yarn to make life more enjoyable.

CREDITS

PUBLISHER AND
CHIEF VISIONARY OFFICER
Jennifer Erbe Keltner

CONTENT DIRECTOR
Karen Costello Soltys

MANAGING EDITOR
Tina Cook

ACQUISITIONS EDITOR
Karen M. Burns

PRODUCTION MANAGER
Regina Girard

INTERIOR DESIGNER
Adrienne Smitke

FRONT COVER DESIGNER
Elizabeth Stumbo

PHOTOGRAPHER
Brent Kane

dedication

To Tom, for your continued, loyal support,
and to our sons, Jeff, John, and Jim

—POLLY

To Bill, who never doubts

—LAURIE

contents

PREFACE

Though distance and age may separate them, the common ground between these two sisters has always been color— blue and white tie them together.

When you first meet Polly Minick and Laurie Simpson, it's the differences between them that you notice. One is outspoken, the other soft spoken. One is strictly a rug hooker, never working with needle and thread; the other is a dedicated quiltmaker, never picking up a hook. For Polly it is always blue and white. For Laurie, it is often blue and white.

But as you get to know these talented sisters better, you begin to see the similarities. Though each of them explores textiles and design through different mediums, their creative intuitions lead them to a shared space—one that is centered around color and composition. It's then that you realize the differences between them are what make their collaboration as a design team work.

Known for their Minick & Simpson designs from Moda Fabrics, they are prolific. Designing more then 40 fabric collections and over 400 rug and quilt patterns between them, their names are familiar to avid textile enthusiasts—both makers

and collectors. What may be less well known is their appreciation for textiles as art in their homes and in their work.

"When we shop for vintage textiles together," Polly says, "I'm always attracted to those pieces that are simple, small, and geometric."

"And I'm looking for things that are graphically appealing to my eye," says Laurie. "If it's quirky and other people think it's a little off, then I'll probably be attracted to it."

Whether you are a maker of classic hooked rugs and quilts, an avid collector of textiles, or simply a lover of the look fiber art can bring to a home, what follows is a trove of ideas and inspiration.

"Living with textiles you love can be simple. Sometimes people overthink things or they value textiles so much that they end up storing them away where no one can see them," Laurie says.

"We'd rather surround ourselves with them," Polly adds, "and create inviting, artful homes."

AMERICANA

*The simplicity of early antiques creates
a stunning setting for textiles.*

The Naples, Florida, home of Polly and Tom Minick is at first glance a study in discipline. Nearly every item in the house is blue or white. But when you get to know its residents better, you begin to understand that it's anything but two-color.

"I think of our furnishings as early antiques. In decorating, some people would call it primitive," Polly says. "But *primitive* also can mean something is broken off or missing, especially from furniture. Some people love the missing part. That's not for me. I like old paint, but I don't want anything missing. I want things that have been loved and used. And once I start collecting a particular item, I have a laser-like focus and an ability to eliminate everything else."

Simplicity and *understated* are two more words that reflect the look of their home. But before going further, it's important to revisit the two-color idea. Between the artful rugs made by Polly and the stunning quilts crafted by Laurie, one commonality emerges: the scrappiness of fabrics used in each. "We figured it out when we started working together," Polly says. "I can't tell you how many rug hookers will hook a sky entirely of one color of wool. Not me. One of my blue-and-white rugs might have 60 or 70 shades of blue in it and 10 or 15 whites. Laurie's quilts contain 50 or more prints. Most people don't see all the different blues, but we see it. Using so many different fabrics adds depth."

Now that you've got your eye out for those many colors, you'll be better able to enjoy the artful, textile-rich Americana home of the Minicks.

OPPOSITE The *LeMoyne Star String Quilt*, handmade by Polly's sister, Laurie Simpson, provides a graphic backdrop for a vignette of antique treasures.

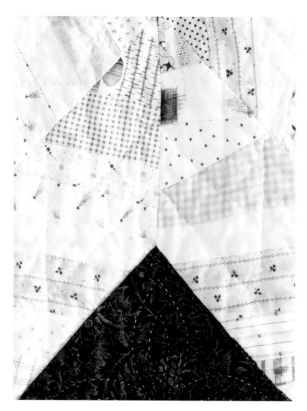

The visual texture shirtings provide is perfect for reproduction quilts. There's enough motif in them to add interest, but not so much they become "spotty."

—LAURIE

ABOVE LEFT AND OPPOSITE Laurie Simpson's hand quilting adds a finishing touch to her *LeMoyne Star String Quilt* that is in keeping with the primitive decor around it. The 18" string stars are composed of eight diamond shapes, each made from a variety of reproduction-print shirtings. **ABOVE RIGHT** Hearts are another favorite motif Polly centers collections around, such as these antique tin candy molds and cookie cutters displayed in a painted tray.

❀ In decor, limiting the color palette puts more emphasis on texture. The pale color shift in the hand-hooked flag rug allows the piece to catch the eye, but it doesn't shout for attention. On the quilt, incorporating navy blue in small measure draws the eye from top to bottom, creating dynamic movement.

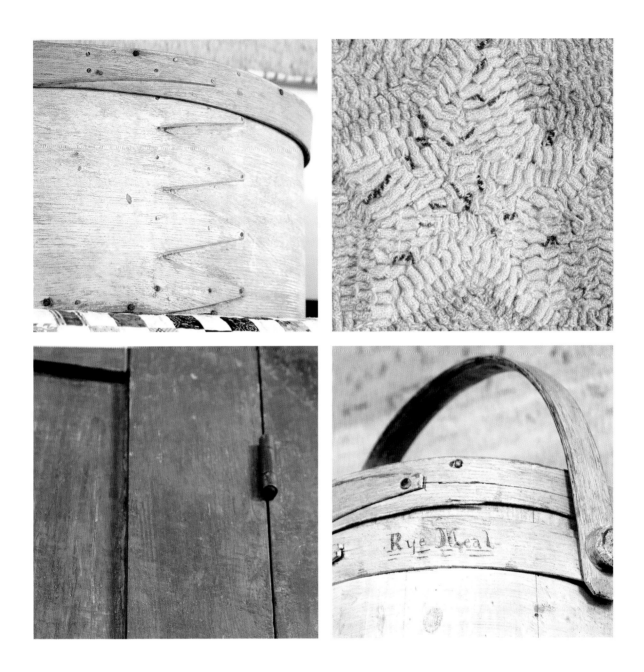

CLOCKWISE, FROM TOP LEFT A Shaker oval pantry box is a juxtaposition of curves and points. Hooking a star with windowpane plaid wool results in scattered blue flecks. A late-1800s firkin was once a utilitarian food storage vessel. A tall, late-1800s jelly cupboard was used by Polly for wool storage for years, but now is used to store dishware.

IRISH CHAIN VARIATION 73" × 91" | *Machine pieced and hand quilted by Laurie Simpson*

❀ "This quilt was inspired by an antique quilt I saw that had big areas of faded fabrics," Laurie says. "Each square is just 1" finished. I collaborated with illustrator Lisa Christensen to graph out the blocks for the quilt so I would be able to re-create that faded look with my fabric placement.

"When choosing fabrics, I looked for blues with lots of open spaces so it would appear as though there were faded openings. I used one white, one navy, and myriad blues. Some of the light blues are so light, they almost appear as white. Others are light blue prints on shirtings."

*Polly's rug designs
are inspired by
her collections*

SPONGEWARE

Kitchen pitchers

GAME BOARDS

Vintage wooden checker
and Parcheesi boards

NAUTICAL ELEMENTS

Wooden sailor whirligigs,
boats, and lighthouses

**SALESMAN'S SAMPLE
BROOMS**

Miniature versions of
kitchen brooms

SAND PAILS

Patriotic tin buckets
made before 1910

HEARTS

Antique candy molds,
cheese strainers, and
cookie cutters

Six of anything qualifies as a collection to me.

—POLLY

LEFT TO RIGHT Tin-heart candy molds, cheese strainers, and cookie cutters; vintage pachisi game board from 1880 (the ancient Indian board game was later known by an American trademark, *Parcheesi*); hand-decorated spongeware kitchen pitcher; salesman's sample brooms (miniature kitchen brooms to scale).

ABOVE When she began rug hooking, Polly incorporated a wider color palette into her work. The painted bowl holding a collection of hooked pieces is a treasured gift from a cousin Polly went antiquing with for many years. **OPPOSITE** Strong or subtle, both color and directional changes add to the visual artistry of the finished rugs.

22 *Blue & White*

KEEP ONLY WHAT YOU TREASURE

A primitive look may mean a sparser number of elements in a room, but it doesn't mean a lack of comforts and treasures.

It's in this sunlit space that Polly does most of her rug hooking, using a quilting hoop in her lap, from the comfort of her chair.

A larger antique game board collection was pared down to only those with strong blue hues. With kids no longer at home, Polly says she had the courage to get white furniture. The blue cupboard is a Ralph Lauren reproduction piece.

Antique and reproduction quilts, draped on furniture and rolled in a basket, soften the overall look of the room.

*When buying antiques, I think of creatively using the pieces
to display textiles—either my rugs or Laurie's quilts.*

—POLLY

ABOVE Original paint is one
requirement Polly sets for herself
in acquiring antiques. Signs of
wear are part of the appeal.

A vintage baby tender (today thought of as a playpen), circa 1820–1840, offers the perfect corral for Polly's collection of blue-and-white quilts, many made by her sister Laurie.

ADVICE FROM POLLY

To create a cohesive look, determine a theme as a starting point.

- **A defined theme** helps focus your effort and your understanding of a specific item's value. "My theme has always been Americana, specifically Americana from the late 1800s, and original painted items. Even though my color palette has changed over the years, my theme has not. I've gone from hunter green, red, and mustard to red, white, and blue (with a bit of gray) to now only blue and white. But having always shopped for Americana means I've kept some pieces for decades."

- **Shop carefully.** "When I first started antiquing, I made the mistake of choosing quantity over quality. I learned after a while to be more selective."

- **Even if your color palette is limited** to two colors, there are still many shades to consider within that palette. "I buy items in several shades of blue, from robin's egg to indigo. But I don't buy blue-green. I like true blues. I collect pieces from cream to white to off-white. I'm not as fussy with whites as I am with blues."

Whether it's Shaker boxes in graduated sizes, square-in-a-square quilt blocks, or hooked stars on a rug, repetition creates a sense of order.

PLEDGE FLAG 45" × 39" | *By Polly Minick*

❀ One of Polly's most enduring and popular designs is her *Pledge Flag* rug. She hooked the classic red-white-and-blue flag design in blue-and-white only once and kept it for her own home.

I put my favorite pieces in the master bedroom. That way, they're the last things I see before I go to sleep and the first things I see when I wake up.

—POLLY

GET THE LOOK

- Include signature items, like the painted wood flag above the bed, that can suit your collection even as your style evolves.

- Built-ins and bookcases can be tricky. Limiting the top two shelves to similar elements simplifies the look.

- To keep your space looking full but not crowded, overlap only a few pieces. Make sure every item has room to shine.

- Mix in some family pieces or treasures with antique finds.

ABOVE The antique doll dress was a gift from Patty Talkington, Polly's cousin, who was also a decades-long antiquing buddy. RIGHT An antique iron house was a Maine antique-show find. "It was white, so it called out to me," Polly says. OPPOSITE The game boards are a mix of reproductions and antiques. "When filling a cupboard, you might have to let go of some of your purest intentions initially," Polly adds.

Some of my rug designs have a more personal story behind them. When I was young, kids decorated veterans' graves at the local cemeteries on Memorial Day, which was at that time called Decoration Day. I had a white bicycle, and off I'd go with a bouquet of fresh flowers to do my civic duty.

—POLLY

DECORATION DAY 38" × 24" | *By Polly Minick*

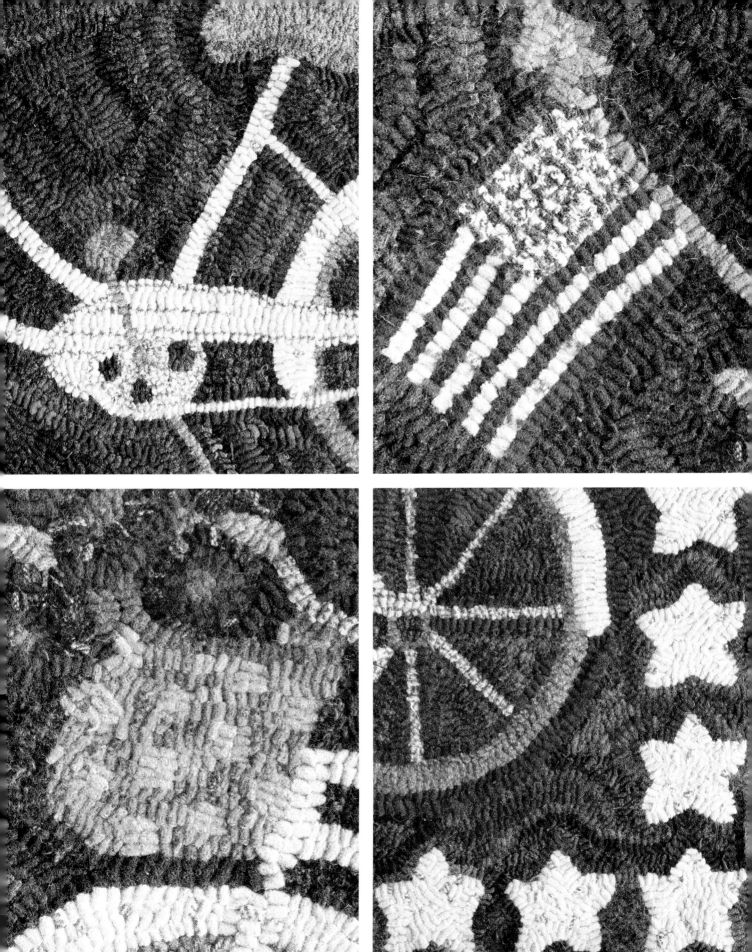

BICYCLE QUILT 66" × 68" | *Hand pieced and hand quilted by Laurie Simpson*

*My quilt is an adaptation of Polly's rug. To me, the most
interesting element is one that's lost until you get up close.
Each star is pieced in a circle, then set into a square.*

—LAURIE

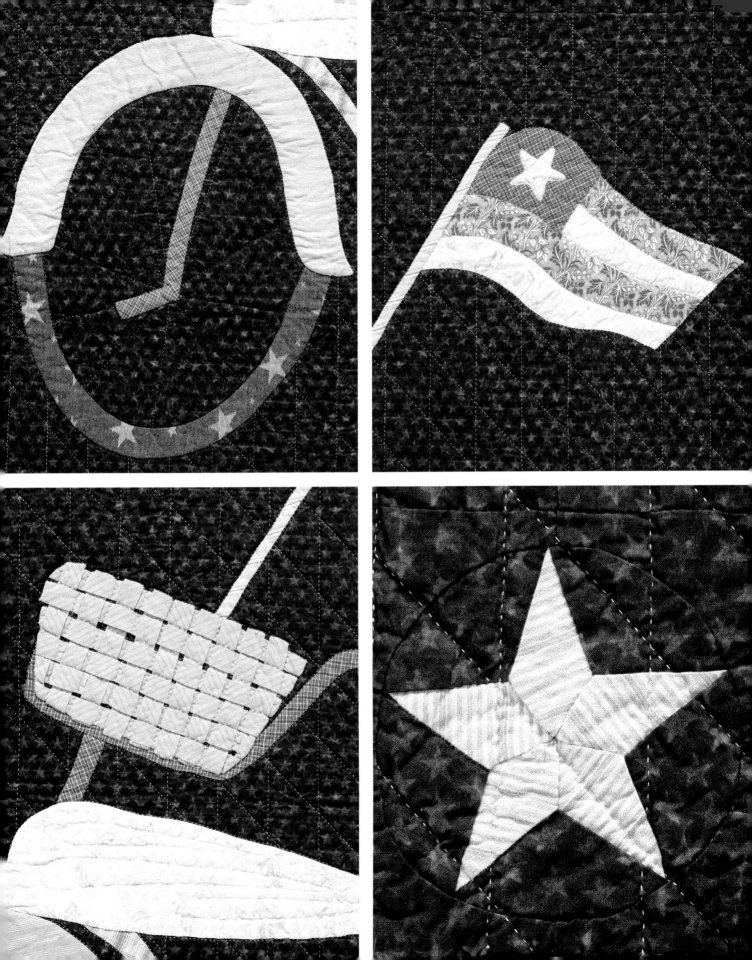

OPPOSITE Graphic game boards inspire both Polly and Laurie—becoming rug designs, as in the 36"-square Pachisi-inspired *Game Board Rug* (detailed above), or quilt patterns. RIGHT The folk-art fish weather vane is a treasured gift that came from a New Hampshire antiques show. "I've always loved it. It's a happy memory for me," Polly says.

Each sister renders her artistry in a different medium—
Laurie with cotton and a needle, Polly with wool and a hook.
Both share a keen sense of color that enables their designs to
transition easily between the two techniques.

NANTUCKET 60" × 60" | *Pieced by Laurie Simpson; machine quilted by Kari Ruedisale*

✿ As pattern and fabric designers, they're known as Minick & Simpson. Polly and Laurie sometimes collaborate to create a quilt and rug combination. "Usually one of us designs something first and the other plays off of that design for a variation," Laurie says.

ABOVE Serendipity was in play when Polly acquired two grocery sacks filled with fabric-strip balls at a Vermont farmhouse auction—opening the sacks revealed that all of the fabrics were blue and white. OPPOSITE Polly's *Irish Chain and Stars* rug is a hooked variation that pays homage to Laurie's *Nantucket* quilt on page 43.

Guests at the Minick home are surrounded by all the textiles and Americana pieces that Polly loves, items that invite a closer look.

SNOW DAY QUILT 67½" × 85½" | *Hand pieced and hand quilted by Laurie Simpson*

❀ "This quilt was my first attempt at monochromatic appliqué," Laurie says. "It's surprising how much realism you can achieve when you're using only value, not color. Experimenting with contrast between fabrics and varying their placement is an essential element in the process.

*Understanding the role that value plays
is important when you're working with a
limited color palette.*

—LAURIE

ABOVE An antique metal horse that was once a Vermont barn's weather vane stands sentry in front of a 41" × 36" flag rug hooked in neutrals. (The rug inspiration came after Polly acquired the neutral wooden flag that hangs above the headboard in the master bedroom, page 32).

OPPOSITE A friend's drawing of a polka-dot horse she'd seen on an antique crock piqued Polly's interest enough that she re-created the look on a wool rug in colors reminiscent of an old crock.

An antique quilt inspired the quilt center. I added my own border design. Look closely at the top—you'll notice the first few bird beaks are open. After stitching those, I made the rest closed. It's a quirk in the quilt that I love.

—LAURIE

INDIGO REVIVAL 54½" × 61½" | *Pieced and appliquéd by Laurie Simpson; machine quilted by Kari Ruedisale*

ABOVE Primitive decor is beautiful in its simplicity.
Appliquéd birds in the quilt's border inspired the
thoughtful pairing of quilt and antique bird cage.

Mounting rugs on a wood frame makes them easier to hang and gives the rug fabric support. The idea began with my Pledge Flag rugs, and now more of my rugs are on the wall than on the floor.

—POLLY

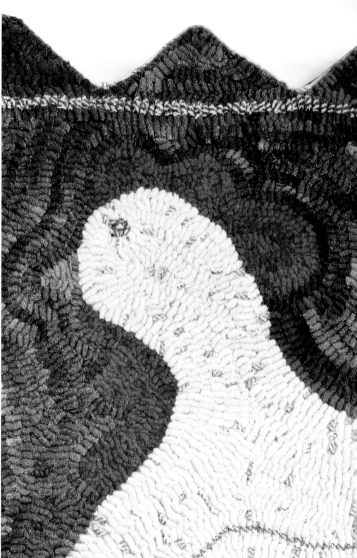

ABOVE Polly has her rugs mounted on a wool-wrapped, wooden frame. The wool is dyed to match the background. This 48" × 28" one-of-a-kind rug hangs in her kitchen, shown on page 55. "I only made one and I liked it, so I kept it for myself." OPPOSITE The striped effect on the blue chicken was achieved by carefully cutting strips along the stripes of houndstooth wool.

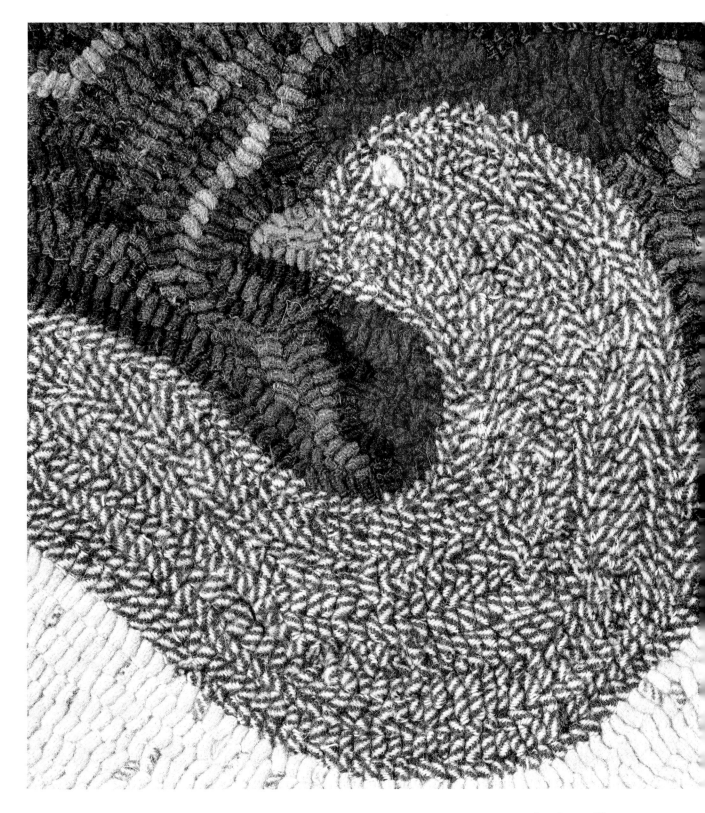

OHIO STAR VARIATION 39" × 39" | *Hand pieced and hand quilted by Laurie Simpson*

❀ Laurie's one-of-a-kind, custom quilts are often the result of inspiration she derives from antique quilts. "I have a library of books at home focused on antique quilts, and there are numerous online resources now where I can pore over incredible vintage quilts," Laurie says. "There are also fabulous quilts to be found in fine-arts museums and even on road trips where I'll accidentally discover quilts in an antique store."

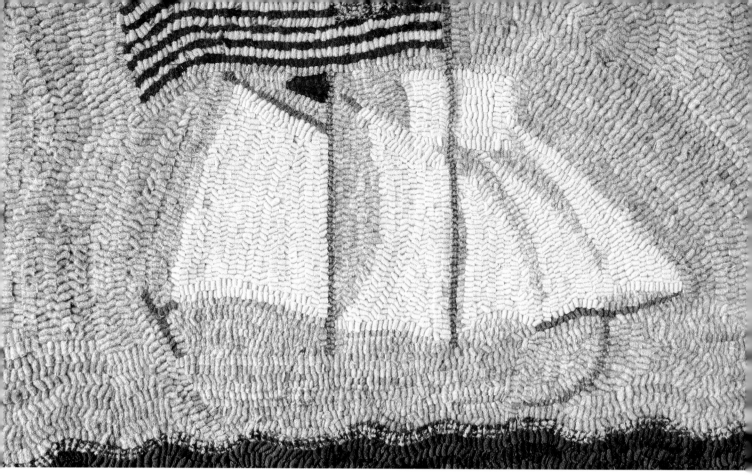

❀ "I started doing more nautical-theme designs when our son, Jeff, was playing summer baseball in the Cape Cod League," Polly says. The area's ships and sea life provided more than enough inspiration for rug designs, along with plentiful painted boats and whirligigs to collect.

Though she was once an avid collector of nautical-themed antiques, only a few pieces remain in Polly's collections today. This sailor is all that remains of her once robust whirligig collection.

COASTAL

*Mother Nature provides all the
blue-and-white inspiration you need.*

If you're lucky enough to live in a space surrounded by blue sky and the lapping shores of the Gulf of Mexico, learning to embrace the coastal look of your surroundings seems the perfect decorating solution. Incorporating wool rugs and quilts may seem a slightly less obvious choice. Fortunately, it's a challenge homeowners Bob and Liz Bulkley embraced wholeheartedly in their Bokeelia, Florida, winter home.

Big fans of Polly Minick's wool rugs, which they discovered at Ralph Lauren's showroom in Naples, Florida, it wasn't long until the homeowners met the artist in person. Collectors of numerous rugs, the Bulkleys expanded their textile collection to include quilts shortly after Polly introduced the couple to her sister Laurie.

Throughout their stunning home, Bob and Liz's love of living with textiles is evident. The picturesque beauty of their surroundings is enhanced by their artful collections. Regardless of whether you're living the dream or dreaming of living in a space like this, the lesson that can be taken away is as follows: Living with what you love and displaying what you love—that's what makes a collector's house a home.

The sky, the sea, and the sand all pay homage to the natural beauty of blue and white as a pairing. This vista provides a breathtaking backdrop for a vintage quilt center, to which Laurie later added an appliqué border.

"In my mind, living the coastal lifestyle means a mix of old and new, lots of nautical things, and the kind of floors you don't mind getting sand on. Don't be afraid to live with vintage things and display them where you can enjoy them. Most older quilts were made for utilitarian purposes and were meant to be used, not put away for safekeeping," Polly says.

Display your favorites over a railing or bannister, if even for a short while, so you can revel in their beauty.

La Playa *is the summer variation of my* Snow Day Quilt
*(page 48). It began as entirely blue and white but, frankly,
was too cold and crisp. It sat unfinished for two years
until I realized it needed a splash of red to warm it up.*

—LAURIE

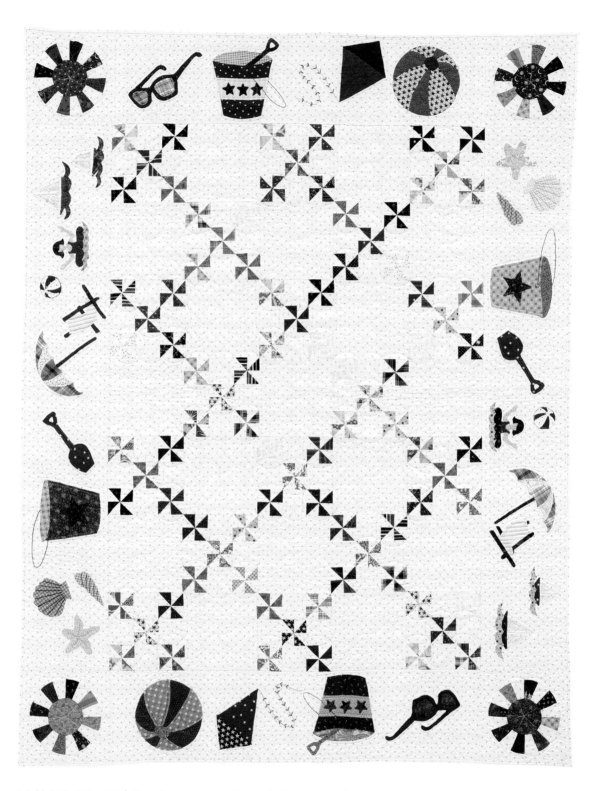

LA PLAYA 63" × 81" | *Pieced and appliquéd by Laurie Simpson; machine quilted by Kari Ruedisale*

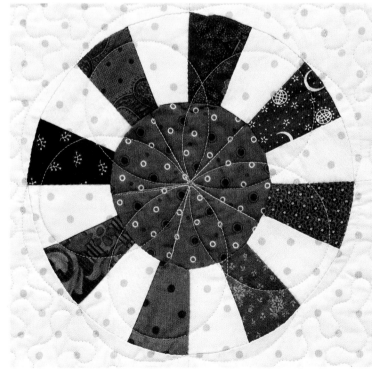

✿ The center of *La Playa* is a play on a traditional Irish Chain quilt pattern in that it repeats Pinwheel blocks rather than plain squares. The sand-pail motifs were the beginnings of the appliqué border, which expanded into other beach motifs as Laurie continued stitching.

BATHING SUIT AND FLAGS 19" × 19" | *By Polly Minick*

❀ Changing directions as she hooks, as well as employing subtle but plentiful shifts in color, enables Polly to achieve depth and movement in her finished pieces.

*Color is so important. If the color isn't pleasing, no one
is going to get close enough to the work to admire it.*

—POLLY

CAPE HATTERAS LIGHTHOUSE
17" × 23" | *By Polly Minick*

BRANT POINT LIGHTHOUSE
17" × 23" | *By Polly Minick*

❀ The inspiration provided by Nantucket lighthouses and others on the
Eastern Seaboard is evident in many of Polly's rug designs. The movement
of sea and sky is attained through Polly's keen instinct for altering direction
as she hooks rugs. "In real life, the Cape Hatteras Lighthouse is black-and-
white stripes," says Polly. "I just color-corrected it for them."

*Whether collecting
or making, unlock
the mystery of what
you love.*

QUIRKS

Are you attracted to the imperfect masterpiece that leaves you asking yourself, "Why did that happen in this piece?"

FAMILIARITY

Building a collection around a few favorite motifs such as stars or birds or flowers ties them together and simplifies the search.

SYMMETRY OR IMBALANCE

Aesthetically, each of us usually prefers one or the other. It doesn't mean you have to limit yourself, but knowing your taste can help you cull items as you search for textiles or patterns.

Hand quilting and hand stitching play quiet supporting roles in the background, allowing appliqué to be the star.

—LAURIE

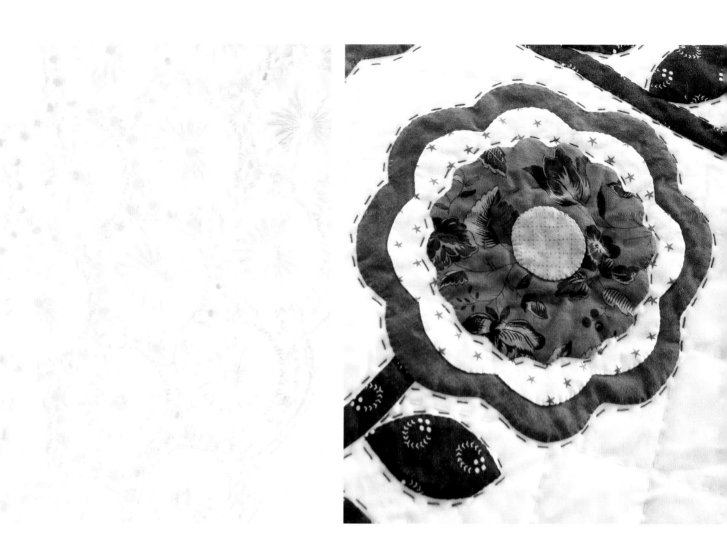

Close-ups of the needle-turn appliqués on the *Austin Bluebird* quilt (page 78) showcase the variety of prints and solid fabrics used. In the master bedroom, the lamp base and linens echo the gentle curves and floral motifs found in the quilt, unifying the decor.

AUSTIN BLUEBIRD 75" × 87" | *Hand pieced and hand quilted by Laurie Simpson*

Polly and I both like sampler quilts from the Ohio Valley region. They feature a hodgepodge of blocks made by different hands in different sizes. When joining blocks, a quilter often had to add Nine Patches or half-square triangles in order to fit all the blocks together. Those quilts were the inspiration for our Austin Bluebird quilt.

—LAURIE

The challenge of marrying warm-climate living with wool textiles might seem to be an insurmountable one. Look to sun, sand, and seaworthy motifs to bridge the gap effortlessly, as shown in this grouping of Polly's hooked pieces—*Mermaid, Beach Gal,* and *Stars and Bars Bathing Suit*—that are among the envy-inducing textile collection on display in the guest room.

The *Beach Gal* rug design was inspired by an antique noisemaker toy (below).

ABOVE The Bulkleys added a splash of fun to the guest bed with a hooked wool pillow featuring the *Stars and Bars Bathing Suit* design.

MERMAID 58" x 24" | *By Polly Minick*

MOBY DICK 42" × 20" | *By Polly Minick*

*Rug hooking is really more about
design and color than technique.*

—POLLY

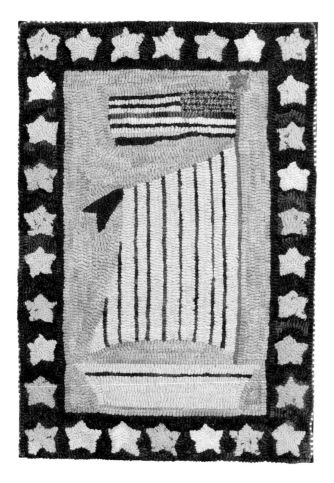

SAILBOAT
17" × 24" | *By Polly Minick*

SEASIDE
29" × 42" | *By Polly Minick*

SAND PAIL/FLAGS AND STARS
19" × 28" | *By Polly Minick*

BOY ON BEACH
27" × 32" | *By Polly Minick*

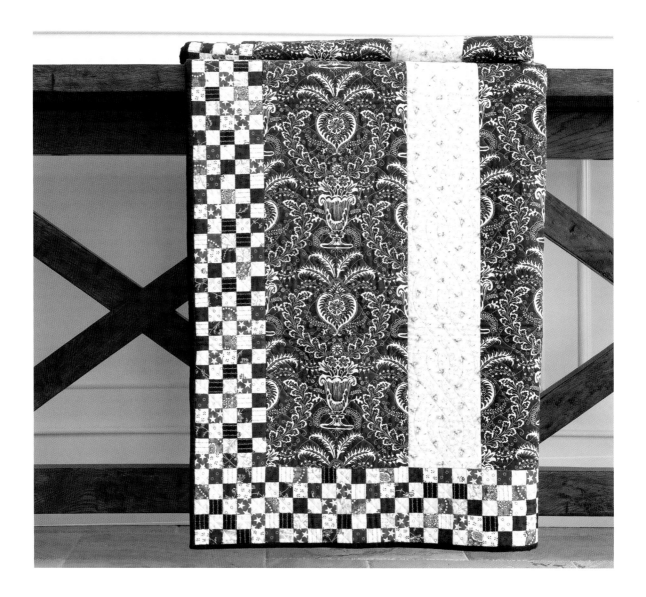

❀ Polly and Laurie design fabric together as Minick & Simpson for Moda Fabrics. Most often, their collections include blue-and-white prints, such as the Indigo Crossing collection featured in this quilt.

"I loved this fabric collection so much, I wanted to see the prints in large pieces, so I created the *Antique Duvet* pattern to show it off," Laurie says. "The prints were reproductions of indigo-resist fabrics from the early 1800s."

When displaying a quilt, look for furniture pieces or architectural elements that repeat design elements in the quilt, such as the Xs formed by the table braces repeating the crosshatch quilting design.

Imagine napping on a gently swinging lounge bed
with a comfy quilt to ward off cool ocean breezes.
In this setting, it's a dream come true.

The quilt showcases Minick & Simpson's Polka
Dots & Paisleys collection.

TOP Here's the view you're treated to, if you don't doze off instantly in the swinging lounge bed.
ABOVE LEFT AND RIGHT The gentle arcs of the quilting mimic the curves of billowy clouds.

SWEET WILLIAM 82" × 82" | *Pieced by Laurie Simpson; machine quilted by Kari Ruedisale*

TEXTILES TELL A STORY

The bandanna prints that form the center of each block are Minick & Simpson fabric reproductions of antique handkerchiefs Laurie acquired from a textile dealer.

"Often, bandannas are thought of as masculine, but the polka dots in those bandanna prints gave them a feminine look," Laurie says. "There were about two dozen polka-dot handkerchiefs in a stack, dated between 1905 and 1920. The woman who owned them had embroidered her monogram on each one, so you know she must've loved them. Knowing what a treasure those kerchiefs were to the woman who owned them, I was inspired to make our reproductions the focal point of this quilt."

❀ Set an artful table by incorporating small textile pieces into your decor. Here, Polly's fish-shaped rug enlivens a tabletop, inviting guests to grab their silverware and a bowl as they prepare to feast on the fresh catch of the day.

The fish rug's design is based on a folk-art fish weather vane at Vermont's Shelburne Museum.

IMAGINE THE STORIES

Laurie shares her views on vintage and folk-art textiles.

- "I love quilts that reveal a hidden story when you look at them closely. What do you think the quilter had in mind?"

- "When asked to describe folk art, I think of two words—*naive* and *untrained*. I appreciate the not-quite-balanced look, and I'm inspired by antique quilts that were made by children. That's the look I wanted to replicate in *Bitty's Quilt* (left), with its make-do background and imperfect shapes."

- "When looking at antique quilt tops that weren't made into quilts, consider this: most often it's because there was an issue. It can be difficult to add something that would finish them, because of whatever that issue is. So, you may want to just enjoy the unfinished top as is."

Back in the day, the only quilting thread available was white. Today, quilters have plenty of colorful options, but it took me a long while to get out of that white box. Using blue thread seemed like a big step.

—LAURIE

There's little wonder as to who Laurie's design muse was for her *Polly's Stars and Stripes* quilt. However, the color palette shown was not its original rendering. The quilt began as a red-and-white beauty before morphing into Polly's always-preferred blue-and-white hues.

BLUE GARDEN 52" × 62" | *Pieced by Laurie Simpson; machine quilted by Kari Ruedisale*

IT'S ALL ABOUT BLUE JEANS

"When people ask me how I choose the mix of blues for a quilt, here's my reply," Laurie says. "Imagine a drawer filled with all the blue jeans you've ever owned—from washed out and faded to brand new. What you'd find in that drawer is a range of colors from light to dark, but still all blue jeans. That's what I have in my mind's eye as I select fabrics. I stay with indigo, but I consider every variation of it, from light to dark.

When it comes to whites or lights, my palette is more forgiving. They could be cream, gray, or ivory. It's sometimes difficult for me to deal with pure white, because it's more contemporary to my eye. But other than that, in my work I like to incorporate just as much diversity in lights."

CLASSIC

*Tradition meets comfort for a
simple yet sophisticated look.*

Classic decorating may have traditional elements at its core, but it doesn't have to be staid or uncomfortable. In fact, most people would agree that a great pair of blue jeans would be considered a classic.

While classic in one sense, much of the blue-and-white decor in Jim and Heidi Minick's Ann Arbor, Michigan, home is as comfortable as your favorite pair of blue jeans. Artful architecture and openings between rooms allow your eye to wander from a comfortable quilt draped over the back of the living room's tweed sofa to a pale hooked-rug flag commanding attention above the office's fireplace mantel just across the entryway. It's clean, fresh, and uncluttered in a classic sense.

Shapes and patterns are familiar ones that have stood the test of time. Textiles, from rugs and quilts to blankets and one-of-a-kind pieces, play an important role in almost every room. And the quintessential color combination of blue and white is right at home in this beautiful space. Fortunately, the homeowners happen to be the youngest son and daughter-in-law of Polly and Tom Minick. Between mother Polly and Aunt Laurie, Jim and Heidi had access to a dynamic textile duo whose expertise they were able to draw on as they transformed their newly renovated house into a home that's both classic and comfortable.

THIS PAGE Texture plays an important role, whether it's the stitches of quilting, the weave of upholstery fabric, or the gridded surface of glassware. **OPPOSITE** "One of the challenges I enjoy most in designing quilts is to take a basic block, like the Hole in the Barn Door used in the *Martin Place* quilt, and change the scale so that it almost looks like something else entirely," Laurie says.

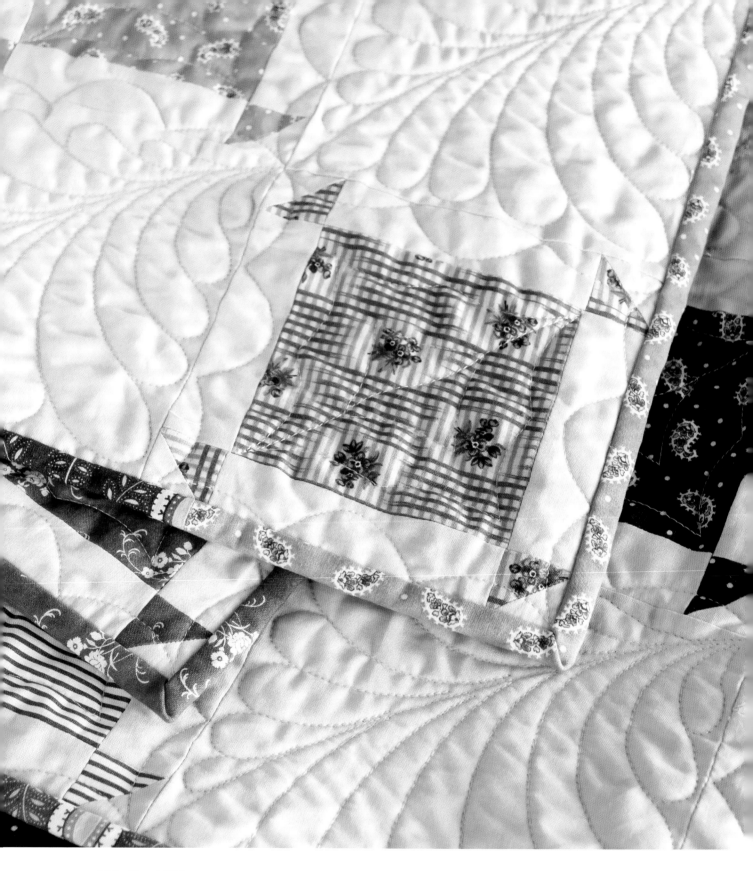

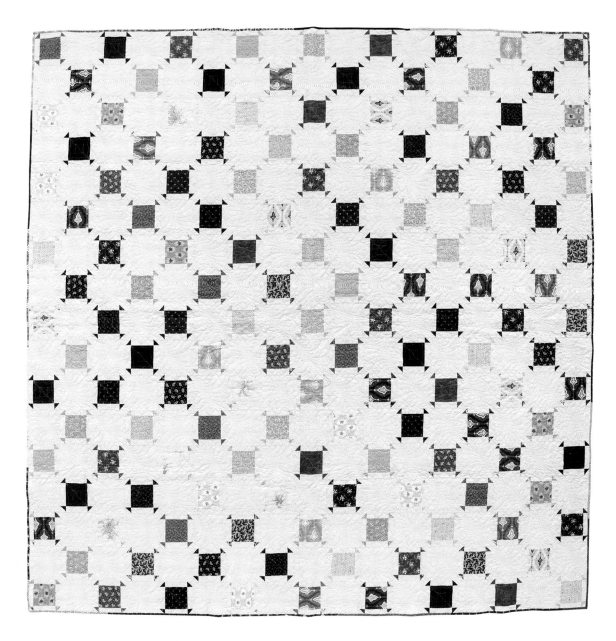

MARTIN PLACE 102" × 102" │ *Pieced by Laurie Simpson; machine quilted by Kari Ruedisale*

Sometimes less is more. The
simplest of wool blankets take
an artful turn when stacked inside
an antique cupboard beneath a
blue-and-white painting.

GET IN THE MIX—ADVICE FROM LAURIE

~ **Reproduction pieces from today** blend well with vintage pieces. "When I was younger, my budget didn't allow for nineteenth-century antiques, so I had to curate my own twentieth-century collectibles. For those who love the thrill of the hunt, finding something new that looks old can be just as exciting as finding a genuine antique."

~ **Combine handmade quilts and linens** with purchased bedding, mixing and matching to suit your needs and showcase your originals.

~ **Don't obsess over matching colors exactly.** "The blues of the quilt and bed skirt don't match, nor do they match the blues on the vintage pillowcase. And yet together they look great. I don't spend a minute trying to match all my blues or whites. I like the organic mix of shades. It makes everything more interesting."

108

What I appreciate most about hand quilting is that the finished quilt is so much softer, it looks older and has such rich texture.

—LAURIE

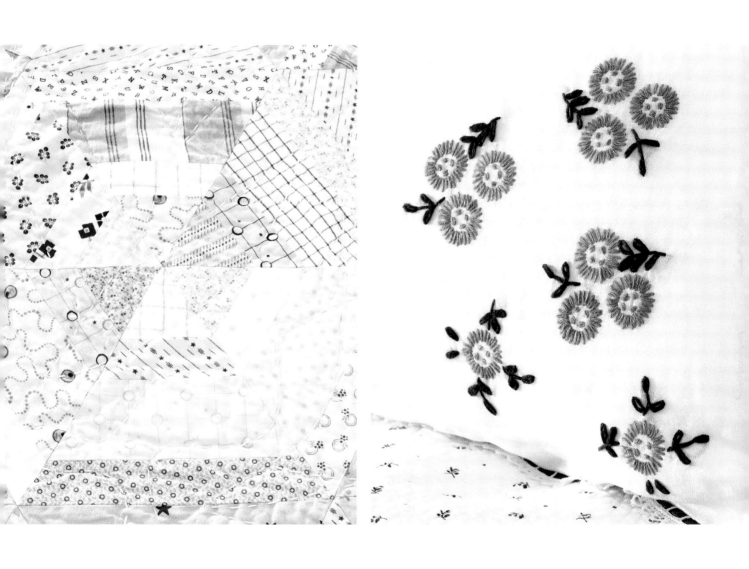

FROM LEFT TO RIGHT Details of the hand quilting in *V is for Victory*, with its scrappy assortment of shirtings and string piecing, are shown along with simple embroidery on a vintage pillowcase.

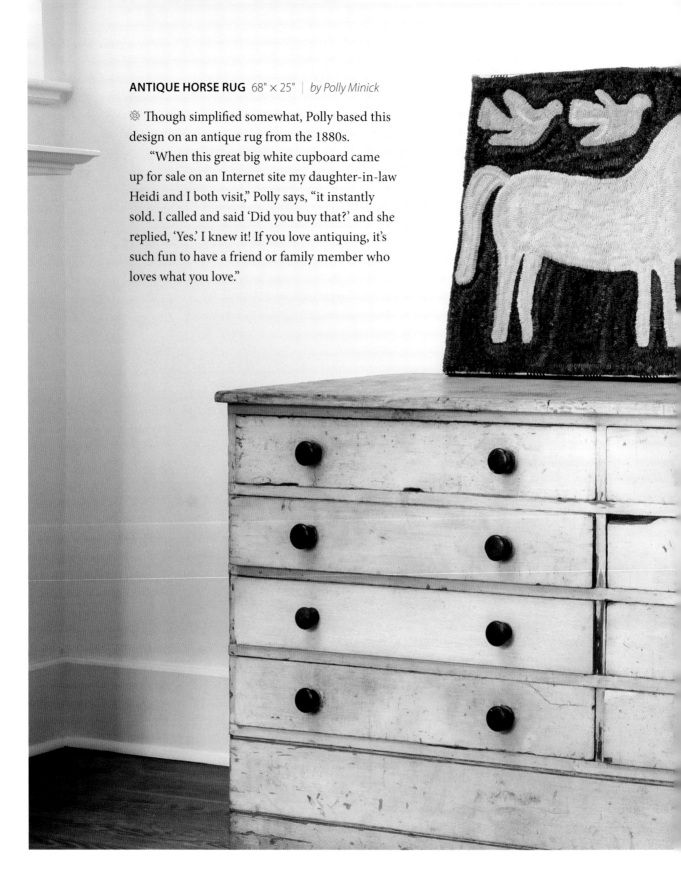

ANTIQUE HORSE RUG 68" × 25" | *by Polly Minick*

❀ Though simplified somewhat, Polly based this
design on an antique rug from the 1880s.

"When this great big white cupboard came
up for sale on an Internet site my daughter-in-law
Heidi and I both visit," Polly says, "it instantly
sold. I called and said 'Did you buy that?' and she
replied, 'Yes.' I knew it! If you love antiquing, it's
such fun to have a friend or family member who
loves what you love."

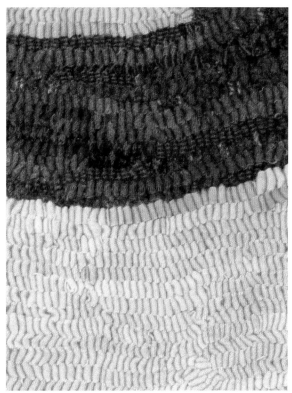

Most people see this rug and think it is two colors—blue and white. They don't realize that there are probably 20 blues and 10 whites hooked into it.

—POLLY

TOP AND RIGHT Artist Rebecca Lindquist asked Polly's permission to render her rug patterns in miniature punchneedle-thread pieces. *Moby Dick* is just 8" × 4." To document her work, Rebecca inserts a tag on the back that lists the original rug pattern's name, designer, and maker. **OPPOSITE** *Old Glory,* just under 6" square, is another of Polly's rug designs that Rebecca rendered in punchneedle.

SECRETS TO A GREAT TEXTILES TREASURE HUNT

- If you love it, it's worth it. You've got to start somewhere, and that's a good place to start. Of course you can do your homework ahead of time to know the value, but sometimes the heart wins over the head.

- Flea markets and antique shops are great places to find discarded textiles, old aprons, vintage clothing, and antique quilt blocks. Remember to look inside of boxes and containers. You never know what treasure may be hidden within.

- Don't limit your finds to only quilts or rugs. Consider collections of vintage fabrics such as homespuns or tickings, table linens, wool blankets, and orphan quilt blocks. Fabric-covered dresser boxes are another favorite of textile collectors.

POLLY'S STARS AND STRIPES 36" × 36" | *By Polly Minick*

❀ "I love the classic clean lines of this kitchen," Polly says. "I try to think like a decorator when I'm making my rugs, keeping them simple and not overly busy, so they'll complement and not compete with everything else in the room."

Unfinished textiles can be unexpected treasures. You needn't worry about staining something that already has some discolorations. Go ahead and use them in your decor.

—POLLY

An antique quilt top finds new life folded on a
table and used as a runner, adding a charming
and rustic look to the tabletop.

SHIP IN NIGHT SKY *32" × 24"* | *By Polly Minick*

❀ Polly's passion for color gets her excited when sharing her thoughts on the importance of using multiple fabrics in a rug or on quilts. "It's all about creating texture and movement," she says. "It looks handmade. No one will ever mistake it or question whether it came out of a factory."

POLKA DOT GARDEN 65" × 74" │ *Hand pieced and hand quilted by Laurie Simpson*

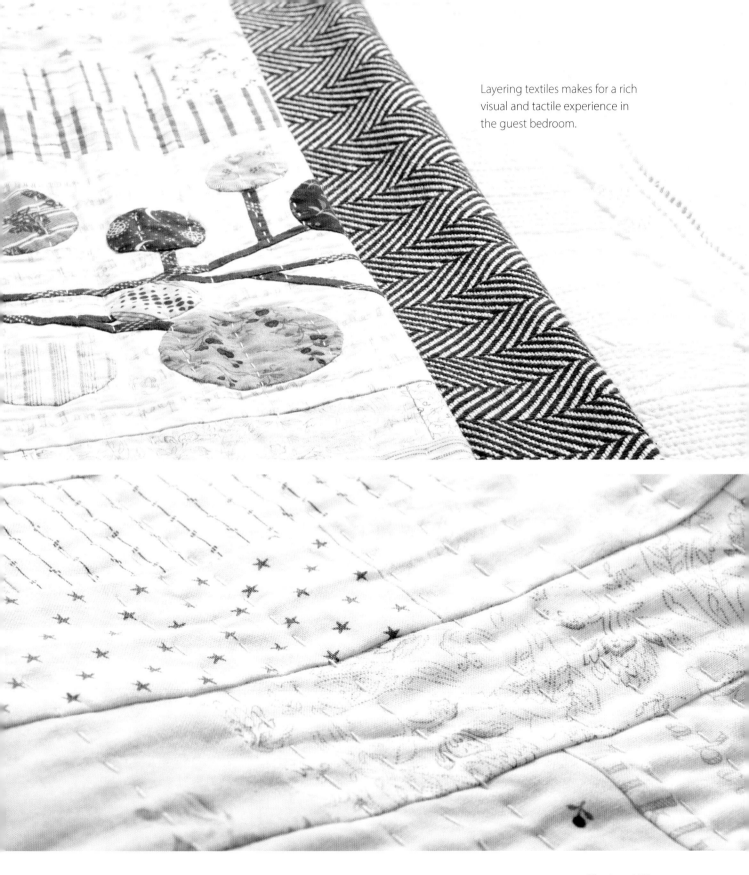

Layering textiles makes for a rich visual and tactile experience in the guest bedroom.

A geometric quilt center with an appliqué border is a favorite look of Polly's. The challenge here was achieving impact using only one color. To succeed, I had to use as many shades of blue as possible for the appliqué animals, oak leaves, acorns, and buds surrounding the center.

—LAURIE

MORNING WALK

*70" x 76" | pieced and appliquéd
by Laurie Simpson; machine quilted
by Kari Ruedisale*

JACK OF THE UNITED STATES OF AMERICA

The Jack of the United States of America is a maritime flag representing US nationality and is flown only at the bow of American vessels that are moored or anchored. The US Navy is a primary user of jacks for its warships.

The blue-fielded, white-starred jack (opposite) is referred to as the Union Jack, not to be confused with the British flag of the same name. This vintage Union Jack, with its 48 stars, would have been in use between July 4, 1912, and July 3, 1959, encompassing both World War I and World War II.

This meaningful and memorable vintage textile is mounted on a canvas frame and proudly displayed in the Minicks' home. Jim Minick is a retired United States Marine Corps colonel.

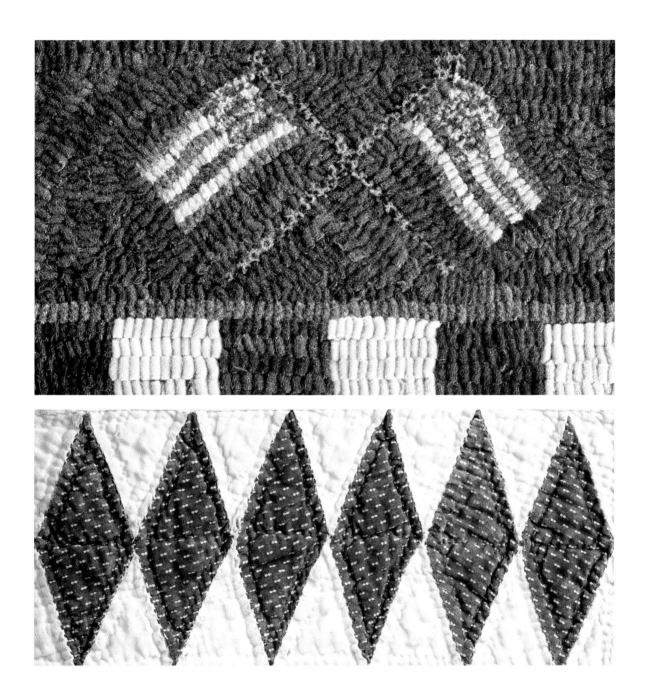

It rarely works to follow someone else's form entirely. You are who you are. Don't try to be anyone else. Interpret ideas for yourself, finding the elements you like.

—POLLY

INDIGO BLUE AND WHITE FLAG 36" × 34" | *By Polly Minick*

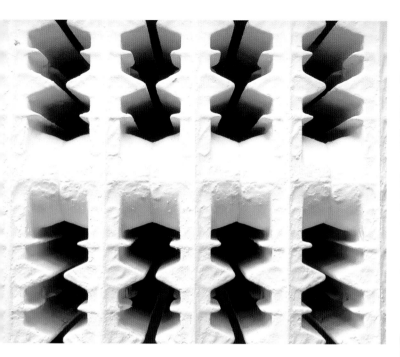

❀ Many of the home's original radiators have decorative designs, such as the arrowheads shown above. It's not difficult to imagine them inspiring future rug or quilt designs.

I'll always have a passion for antique quilts. Their scrappiness and make-do quirks just speak to me. And I appreciate a great quilt pattern, like this one by Karen Styles, that enables me to reproduce an antique quilt using today's fabrics and techniques.

—LAURIE

MRS. BILLINGS COVERLET
94" × 94" | *Antique reproduction pieced and hand quilted by Laurie Simpson; pattern design by Karen Styles for Somerset Patchwork & Quilting*

Polly Minick

I STARTED MAKING RUGS IN THE 1970s. As a wife and mom to three young boys, I loved antiquing and I'd see rugs at antique shops, but I couldn't afford to buy them. So I figured I could make them myself, and I enrolled in a continuing-education class to learn how to rug hook. When it came to getting supplies, if I needed red, I went to the thrift store and I'd buy a red wool skirt to cut into strips. In the end, my rugs just weren't looking as I'd hoped they would.

At the time I also was working and went on a business trip to Texas. I was just 45 minutes from a house that had been featured in *Country Home* magazine, so I went to see it. On her property, the homeowner had an antique shop. It turned out she also hooked rugs. She had cupboards full of muted soft wool, colors that I just didn't have or couldn't find to work with. So I asked her, "How did you get that?" She told me there were a couple people around the area who dyed wool. I bought the hand-dyed wool on the spot, and that started me on the path to working with a colorist so that I, too, could have beautiful wool.

I'm a lifelong antiques fanatic who loves original paint and Americana. In textiles, I like simple designs, small motifs, and geometrics. I've probably made more than 400 rugs in my lifetime, each one a labor of love.

Laurie Simpson

WHEN I WAS 14 YEARS OLD, I saw a quilt in *Woman's Day* magazine and I wanted it. There were no quilts or quilters in our family at that time, and probably only one or two books in the library on the subject of quiltmaking. But I rode into the city and went to Kresge's store and bought an eighth yard of everything—polyesters, flannels, silks. The store clerks quickly learned to know me and to run the other way when I showed up. I was a self-taught quilter who never took a class. I borrowed a neighbor's sewing machine to piece that first quilt together. I used a polyester sheet for the backing. Everyone told me it had to have yarn ties to hold it together (though I couldn't see any in the magazine picture). So, I tied my quilt together with yarn.

I've come a long way since that first quilt. I've probably made more than 300 quilts in my lifetime. I prefer to do everything by hand—the piecing, appliqué, and quilting. I love blue and white, and our Minick & Simpson fabric lines for Moda are almost exclusively red, white, and blue. But truth be told, I live in a more diverse, colorful home than my sister Polly. I love orange, as you might gather by the glimpse you get into my sewing studio. And my all-time favorite color is the red-orange you see in vintage Fiestaware.

Special Thanks

FAR LEFT The Americana section was photographed in the home of Tom and Polly Minick in Naples, Florida. Thank you, Tom, for moving furnishings and other items at our every whim as we worked our way from room to room, always needing "just one more thing."

CENTER The Coastal section was photographed in the home of Bob and Liz Bulkley in Bokeelia, Florida. Avid collectors of textiles, Bob and Liz provided a stunning seaside setting for this book. Special thanks to Bob and Liz for opening their home to our team. Your generosity in sharing your beautiful home to showcase our blue and white textiles is greatly appreciated.

RIGHT The Classic section was photographed in the home of Polly and Tom's youngest son and his wife, Jim and Heidi Minick. Though the homes of any of Polly's three sons—Jeff, John, and Jim—could have been featured, Jim and Heidi are fortunate to live in the same town as Jim's aunt, Laurie Simpson, whose studio was also photographed. Having just moved into their Ann Arbor, Michigan, home a couple months prior to our team's arrival, Jim and Heidi were beyond gracious in allowing us access to their incredible home and the treasury of textiles within.

Resources

Many of the textiles throughout this book are one-of-a-kind or vintage pieces from the artists and/or homeowners. However, several Polly Minick rugs and Laurie Simpson quilts have patterns available (see listing below of patterned pieces and the page on which they appear). Many can be found through minickandsimpson.blogspot.com or online at animblethimble.com. You may also find patterns for a variety of works in previously published books, including: *The Americana Collection: Hooked Rugs* (Martingale, 2007); *American Summer: Seaside Inspired Rugs and Quilts* (Kansas City Star Books, 2012); *Everyday Folk Art: Hooked Rugs and Quilts to Make* (Martingale, 2005); *Quilts and Rugs* (Quiltmania, 2013); *Victory Girls: Patriotic Quilts and Rugs of WWII* (Kansas City Star Books, 2011).

"It is important to express oneself...provided the feelings are real and are taken from your own experience."

—BERTHE MORISOT,

1841–1895, FRENCH IMPRESSIONIST PAINTER